I0766289

Beyond Habit

Exercises to Cultivate Your Creative Writing in a Month

Kate Forth

For Rosie,

For Lizzie,

For Matt,

Your stories are my favourite ones of all.

AN OPEN LETTER

Dear Reader,

I thought we had best start with a quick tale.

Just over a year ago I had a particularly unwelcome realisation: I was an ex-writer. This calamity happened gradually as busy weeks merged into dreary, wordless months. Without me realising, the writerly part of me had become hidden away; slowly writing became just a memory of a life that had gone.

Of course, I scribbled ideas and the occasional sentence or verse. But I ignored the garish truth. To continue to improve my output I needed to not only write but to practice. I knew this. I'd chosen to study creative writing at postgraduate level. I got it. But somewhere in between the moment that I received my MA and finally got my head around being responsible for a small human, the time for practicing had become subsumed elsewhere and I hadn't fought for it, even when I'd wanted too.

There is no excuse grand enough to really explain this period. For eighteen months I had felt guilt about not working on 'the novel'. I couldn't. Of course, I couldn't. In fact, it was a red herring. I had given myself the opportunity to recognise my talents and failings when it came to the written word. I had exercised the parts of myself that find joy in cadence and pace, rhythm and word play. I had not been writing *anything*.

Rather than the raging storm of creativity I'd hoped for, a lull began, both in my education and my usual love for experimentation, leading to a lack of growth and development as a writer. I had not done a single thing to allow me to improve. Something needed to change, and I realised that committing to 500 words a day was not where I needed to start. I needed practice.

Lots of practice.

And, without any judgment or conceit, every other writer does too.

Yours,

Kate

1

ARE YOU A WRITER?

Clichés and caricatures of writers may be coloured with notions of tortured souls and recluses, of adventurers and beret-wearers, of overnight millionaires and 'every-one-has-a-book-in-them'-ers. But what happens when you really think about that all-important question: What makes a writer? What is the *only thing* that makes a person a writer – that makes *you* a writer?

A writer is someone who writes.

And like with any hobby, talent, or vocation, writing does not arrive as a fully-formed skill, as a bird takes to flight. It doesn't care how busy you are or let up because of experience.

Whether you are new to the word-count brigade, are stuck in a *little* rut, or have accidentally abandoned writing and are much more likely to be found arguing with yourself about such things as, 'just one more episode/tweet/cuppa…' or 'How can I write when I do not have the *correct* notebook?', this book is for you. It has been created by a writer for writers at all levels who are ready to accept that they need to make a commitment to improvement.

Beyond Habit is not a 101 guide on how to write a novel or 365 days of writing prompts. It is a book filled with a full 31-day selection of exercises that will give you the opportunity to explore your imagination, make mistakes, and recognise any go-to themes, scenarios or ideas.

Beyond Habit is also not here to get you to focus on your writing dreams and ambitions. Cherish those but let them go to the back of your mind for now. Whether your dream is that you want just one of your novels to exist as a completed manuscript, or as big as wanting to make a more than healthy living from your work, that is not what we are concentrating on here. If you can get your daily habits right, your long-term dreams may well follow. We are going back to basics – if you have big writing aspirations then I am hoping that above all else you want to be the best writer that you can possibly be. That was my ambition when I learned to do these exercises for myself. That is the purpose of this book.

After all, an artist will sketch each and every day. Can you imagine a musician who is not dedicated to playing their instrument daily? Writing deserves the same amount of dedication because, second only to being a person who writes, a writer is someone devoted to storytelling.

So why am I suggesting that you don't just spend time each day on your work in progress? Well, because that is your work and because writing every day should be not only about constantly upping your word count. It should be about refining your skills and knowledge. Refine them and your work will develop. This is not only necessary for new or as-yet-unpublished writers. Whether for your personal enrichment or for professional development, it is an inescapable daily requirement. It is part of the job.

Each task in this book will allow you to experiment, have fun, work outside of your comfort zone, and ultimately emerge with more skill and confidence as a writer. I know because it is how I brought myself back from the writer's graveyard.

Committing to these daily Beyond Tasks has an end goal - to make *you* a *better* writer.

Beyond Tasks should not seem like a chore, even if that is how writing has seemed to you lately. As they flex your writing mind, you should begin to recognise your successes. There will be the day when you complete an exercise, go to close the notebook and notice a small but beautiful phrase in the middle of your page and wonder where it came from. Those are the moments when you will appreciate just how important the art of improvement is. These are your *beyond* moments.

Of course, this is also likely to have a positive effect on your writing routine and we are not going to ignore that. I know these tasks are not the only writing you'll want to undertake each day so, when you start, you will see that each day also suggests a bonus exercise for your work-in-progress that will relate the lesson of a daily exercise to your ultimate goal. You won't only learn, you'll learn to use your new habits.

Before all else though, commit to completing the daily writing practice every day. It should only take a maximum of twenty minutes – although being inspired and writing beyond is actively encouraged. Some tasks may take you mere moments. Make a promise to yourself NOW to spend the next 31 days completing the Beyond Task and revel in your growing capabilities and your expanding imagination.

2

SOME COMMON SENSE

I've already given you the golden rule: PRACTICE WRITING EVERY DAY. *Beyond Habit* is the perfect place to start that journey. But, just in case you're still feeling a bit overwhelmed by the prospect of that much commitment, here are ten other habits that will help you along the road to becoming a better writer.

Read Widely

Try to read every day, even if it is just fitting in a cheeky chapter during your coffee break. Try to vary what you read. If you can, aim for a book a week (so four a month) from any of the following:

- A book in your favourite genre or by a loved author.
- A non-fiction book.
- A book you would never usually consider reading.
- Something someone else has recommended to you.

Carry a notebook and pen

Two notebooks if possible: one for lines, phrases and ideas that pop into your head and a second for observations.

Get up twenty minutes earlier

This gives you twenty extra minutes every day and eliminates any excuse for not having time for your Beyond Task. Whether you use the time during your breakfast to complete the task, or it gives you an extra burst of energy in the morning to straighten up the kitchen before you leave for work, you have twenty minutes in the bank for some time in the day to write.

Be present

Have experiences. From travelling to engaging in a conversation with someone new, experience will swell your empathy and imagination, both of which will help immeasurably when it comes to your writing. Being present in life provides your own personal wealth of inspiration that will be totally unique to you.

Be critical

The ability to recognise things in others' work (and storytelling is in play within every art form) that are successful and unsuccessful, obvious or subtle, thematic or engaging, will also help you to be subjective when it comes to editing and being critical of your own work and will challenge you to write beyond a simple sentence.

Pay attention to current affairs

From the important news in the political sphere to celebrity gossip to human interest stories, being aware of the social and cultural world around you is a great way to recognise themes or meaning in your work. Reflecting on how these issues affect you or the emotional response that you have to them will help you develop convincing plot and character points.

Live well

From eating healthily to getting outside, keeping your body in good order will help to keep your mind that way too. Try to walk at least ten minutes each day without using this time for anything in particular. Maybe those ten minutes will help you press the reset button for the rest of the day or maybe the quiet time will help you to make sense of a plot point or a missing word that has been eluding you.

Embrace airplane mode

Personally, I use pen and paper for as much of my writing as possible but if you prefer to type from the off, disconnect yourself from the internet to avoid any distractions whilst you work. If you have a research query, write it down. It is far better to dedicate time to researching the question thoroughly later than interrupting your writing when you're in flow.

Schedule time

Remember those twenty minutes we added to your day earlier? That is my way of gifting you time to complete your Beyond Task and if that is all you are doing for now, we are good to go. But if you are looking at making writing a significantly larger part of your day, you need to look at your routine to see where you can make changes. Is your lunch break long enough to fit in half an hour of writing? Do you have time in the evening that could become writing time?

Make space

It does not need to be a library-inspired study, lined with bookcases with a large oak desk looking out of a window. Indeed, I truly believe that if needs must you *can* write *anywhere*. But I can also see the benefit for a creative mind of having that space all of your own. If you have a spare room, great! Or maybe you have an alcove where you can fit a small desk or a writing bureau. Wherever you can fit in a place to write, make it yours. Of course, this is not fundamental to your Beyond Tasks but when it comes to a work-in-progress, a tidy place to sit and work will be good for you.

COMMON DISTRACTIONS

In total fairness, these are distractions that infiltrate daily life regardless of who you are and what you do. But, right now, you are someone displaying a commitment to their craft. Why not write a personal list of ten reasons that you don't write? By recognising where your time really goes you can start to take control and ensure that your writing time is well organised and protected. Ten common ones would be:

1. Social Media.
2. Household chores.
3. Worrying.
4. Binge watching box sets.
5. Expectations from friends and family.
6. Fretting about clutter.
7. Clicking your way through the Internet (or 'research').
8. Checking your phone.
9. Putting the kettle on.
10. Using all of the above as an excuse.

So why have I pointed out a glut of ways that you might waste time every day? It really isn't to make you feel guilty – I do these too! They are part of modern day-to-day life and by no means do I expect you to go cold turkey with any of them. (Well, maybe with number 10!)

But these are *all* things that could easily distract you from writing and you could probably add ten more to the list. By controlling time spent on social media, or setting aside a specific time to speak to your loved ones, you should be able to easily open an opportunity to create. Remember, the starting point here is only asking for twenty minutes and you know you can easily find it if you cut out just some of those things on that list.

Sometimes *one more episode* will be the priority. But your story must come first or you'll never know how *that* novel ends.

4

EQUIPMENT

For completing the Beyond Tasks

- A notebook dedicated to Beyond Tasks only.
- Pens or pencils, according to your preference.

For ALL writers

- Dictionary (not online).
- Thesaurus (not online).
- Library card.
- Computer with word processing programme.
- Envelope files.
- Printer.
- Printer paper.
- A notebook for planning.
- A notebook for observations.
- A notebook for ideas.

Optional extras:

- A teapot or flask.
- Dictaphone.
- A cork board for inspiration.
- A water bottle and bowl of fruit.
- A clock with an alarm.

A writing exercise for every day

HOW TO USE THIS BOOK

On the following thirty-one pages you'll find a 'Beyond Task' and an 'Extra Task' for each day.

For the first month that you use this book, commit to doing the writing exercise outlined in the Beyond Task. If you're still up for writing after that, the Extra Task comes in to play.

The Beyond Tasks are varied, simple writing exercises that are designed to be repeated as often as you like. They will get you to think about the world around you and explore new and exciting ways to define the world and its intricacies.

One of the best things about these exercises is that they only have one purpose: to make you practice writing. It is through this practice that I hope you will begin to grow confidence in the details that you notice, the language that you choose, and the themes that you return to time and time again.

Remember, you are not committed to them, though I do hope that there are moments of inspiration littered amongst them for yourself. Keep them, refer to them.

And once the month is up, repeat them. Repeat all of them if you wish or, if one task speaks to you as a writer, choose that, choose your writing self, but whatever you do, keep practicing.

The Extra Tasks are just that – an optional extra. Each one is designed to help you plan, or explore, your work in progress and create your own resources for your fantasy world, in enjoyable and enlightening tasks that will familiarise yourself with your story, help you to fix plot holes, and to understand the wider world of your novel, both within its pages and in the themes and questions that have inspired your work in the first place.

Now, if you've got this far, what's another ten minutes? Go!

Day One

The Beyond Task

Observe your environment

Think about a journey you are familiar with, either from your past or present.

Write a paragraph taking yourself on the journey. Focus on describing the things that you would see.

Now, either take that journey, or search your memory for times that the journey was slightly different. Maybe someone was usually with you? Or you saw something unusual happen? Maybe something that was there has long since disappeared?

Write a new paragraph with these details.

Now, can you combine them into one paragraph?

The Extra Task

Telling and Retelling

Write a single sentence that tells your story/work in progress.

Write a paragraph that tells your story/work in progress.

Now, write a page that tells your story.

These three different retellings are a brilliant way to keep focus. They will help you to be able to understand the bare bones of your current project and are a fantastic resource for your planning and research notes.

Day Two

The Beyond Task

Flash Fiction

What were you doing at 10.00am yesterday morning? Think about the actions you were performing, the place that you were, what you could hear and jot them down.

Now write a 400-word flash fiction short story. Try to keep focussed on the sensations that you experienced and what was going on around you whilst you performed your task.

The Extra Task

Do I Know You?

Keeping track of your characters and their relationships can be tricky when you first start writing.

Write down the names of all your main characters and cut them out so you have a piece of paper per name.

Pick a character and lay their name down in front of you. In turn, take each remaining character and lay their names next to each other. Then, write the following about their relationship:

1. Does character A know character B? How?
2. What does character A think of character B?
3. What does character B think of character A?
4. What is the defining moment/scene between these two characters in your book?

Repeat this process until you have paired up all the characters. This process helps you to get to know your characters better, especially as you will be having to think about them through each other's eyes. It also creates a handy resource for continuity.

In the instance that character A and B don't know each other, you can still go through the subsequent questions by writing about what they *would* think of each other.

Day Three

The Beyond Task

People and Things

Pick five things that you can see. Invent a character who would own, use, or throw away these items. Why? How do they relate to their history or personality? Jot down your ideas.

Pick one of the objects and write a sentence or two to describe an emotional response to it.

How would your character react to the loss of that object? Write a short monologue (a page or so) of their reaction. Use the ideas that you noted about their relationship with all the objects to inform the response throughout the monologue.

The Extra Task

Change the Form

Write a poem about the setting of your opening chapter. Aim for approximately 40 lines.

Focus on the imagery of the place and the way that you have imagined it. Close your eyes and think about even the smallest details – you'll be surprised what you see!

Day Four

The Beyond Task

Eavesdrop

Close your eyes and listen. List every sound that you notice.

Choose one and write ten different ways to describe it.

The Extra Task

Skills

What is your protagonist's defining skill? Create a presentation about their ability that they could deliver to an audience. Think beyond what they have done, or will do, in the story. Is it a natural talent, or a learned skill? Do they enjoy or resent it? What mistakes have they made along the way?

You can repeat this for other characters to create a database of their attributes and abilities.

Day Five

The Beyond Task

Knock, Knock

Imagine that you have discovered a door in a wall that you have never noticed before and feel compelled to knock. Nobody answers. Write a paragraph about how you feel about finding the door, and it not being answered.

Then imagine you knock again and the door opens. What do you find behind the wall? Write a stream of consciousness for ten minutes about your discovery.

The Extra Task

Step by Step

Write out your plot in chronological order, from the beginning in terms of time (not the order of your narrative). For example, put a flashback that appears in Chapter Eight in to the correct timeline order. Now order those points to correspond with the narrative chronology you have been working with.

Next, play around. What would happen if certain events were to be shown before or after you intend to reveal them? Can you see any holes in your plot that need to be filled? How do your subplots fit into the story as a whole? Do they have their own narrative order?

Day Six

The Beyond Task

Right and Wrong

What was the last argument you had? Write down a few points about it. Who was it with? What was it about? Were you frustrated? Upset? Pig-headed? Did you get your point across? Did you feel that it was resolved?

Now, in any form you wish, from poem to script, newspaper article to opening chapter, write about the argument. Why not write in the third person to add depth to both sides of the argument?

The Extra Task

The Motivation

Pick three characters from your story. Ask them one question: 'Why?'

Explore, in any form you feel fits, from interior monologue to sestina, why their behaviour is as it is in your story. What is driving their actions? What do they wish to achieve, and ultimately, what resolution are they likely to get in the narrative? Is the ending you are going to give them the same as the ending they would like?

Day Seven

The Beyond Task

Egotist

Write your own 'About Me' text using a 'pyramid' technique. Remember to write in the third person.

Aim for about 500 words using the following as a guide:

1. A short, punchy sentence to introduce who you are.
2. Paragraph 1: Recent achievements, publications, competition successes etc.
3. Paragraph 2: Training and education.
4. Paragraph 3: Recent work and current projects.
5. Paragraph 4: Elaborate on your personal life with all the things that make you memorable and interesting. (interests, skills, travel, languages, hobbies)

The Extra Task

Read All About It!

Read back the last few pages of your work in progress. Pick out a key element from the plot (or poem!). Write a short piece in the style of a newspaper or magazine article. Keep it factual but be as creative with the details as you like.

Read it back. Have you added in any new perspectives? Facts? Has it made a small plot point larger? Could you use that to improve your recent work?

Day Eight

The Beyond Task

The In-Crowd

Think about someone that you interact with daily but do not know outside of that situation. Write up to 750 words of your interaction from their point of view as an interior monologue.

The Extra Task

Doodlin'

Look at your novel plan for the next scene or chapter that you will be writing (but haven't started yet). Instead of writing, construct a film storyboard treatment. Don't worry about your drawing skills – stickmen will do if necessary! – but do try to add as much detail as you can. If you've imagined it, *draw* it. From frown lines to speeding cars, cold breath hanging in the air to chirping bird, visually bring the story to life. Add in the background details that you imagine when writing. Is it dark? Are there trees? Think about all the things that you have drawn; what would it feel like, smell like, sound like?

Now use the storyboard to write the first paragraph. Use the images that you have drawn as your guide. Try to focus on adding in all the details, however small, that you have drawn. Is there a way to weave them in? Remember, you've *shown* with the drawings, the writing is the time to *tell*.

Day Nine

The Beyond Task

Mundane to Magnificent

Choose someone from this list: Olympian, Eldest Sibling, Drama Teacher, Receptionist, Courier. And something from this list: Tent Pegs, A Broken Sink, A Padlock, An Old Car Battery, Pen Drive.

Write 100 words about A using B.

Write 100 words about A losing B.

Write 100 words that combines A using and losing B.

Choose a second character from the first list. Pitch your two As against each other as they search for B.

The Extra Task

Reproduction Line by Line

Pick a random book from a bookshelf. Open it on any page. Choose a paragraph or so. Dissect each sentence into its components, e.g. pronouns, verbs, prepositions, adjectives, etc.

Rewrite the paragraph with your own characters and story, following the same lexical structure.

Day Ten

The Beyond Task

True Story

Pick a story from a newspaper or magazine. Highlight the key details. Using the key details, write a poem about the story. Try to balance imagery with a consideration of the emotional responses you have had to those key elements to create texture in each line.

The Extra Task

Wakey, Wakey

Your character wakes up in their bed. What time is it? What is the first thing they do? What are their plans for the rest of the day?

Write for ten minutes in the first person present as they get up (or stay in bed!). Intertwine their actions with their thoughts and emotions about what has happened, what is happening, and what they expect – or hope – will come to pass.

Day Eleven

The Beyond Task

Beautiful Simplicity

Write a haiku

A haiku follows this pattern:

Line 1: 5 syllables

Line 2: 7 syllables

Line 3: 5 syllables

The Extra Task

(Maybe) Kill Your Darlings

What would happen if you put your protagonist into mortal danger? (If they will face, or have faced, peril choose a different hazardous situation.) How would they cope with the idea of death facing them?

Write the monologue that you think they would give in this situation.

Day Twelve

The Beyond Task

Metaphors

Write a metaphor for each of these abstract nouns:

Truth
Hatred
Stupidity
Delight
Power
Stillness
Death
Memory
Rumour

The Extra Task

Dear Diary,

Start a new journal to record your thoughts and feelings about your writing process.

Write about what you have written today and how you felt about writing today. What did you find easy? What did you struggle with? Did anything seem problematic? Do you have any issues that you need to address? What would you like to achieve tomorrow?

Day Thirteen

The Beyond Task

I Must Confess

Write a letter to someone about something that you wish you had told them. It doesn't have to be a deep or dark secret, nor a major declaration of love – unless you would like it to be! Aim for a page. Format it formally. Balance the facts with the feelings. Explain why you did not tell them this before.

(And don't forget to dispose of the evidence if you don't really want to get found out!)

The Extra Task

Places for People

Create (or reuse if you've kept them) two sets of flashcards; one with the names of all your characters, and the second with the locations you are using in your novel.

Pair each location and character in turn. From their perspective, write a response to this place. It can be as simple as a single word or a longer piece of prose.

The Beyond Task

Cliffhangers

Spend fifteen minutes writing a short story. Pause for a moment. Read it over

Now add a cliffhanger ending. This could be:

- A character reacting to something unexpected.
- A character making an unexpected decision or taking a surprising action.
- A sudden change to the situation.
- A new character arrives.

The Extra Task

Five Minutes to Change Your Life

For the next five minutes write, whether in list form or stream of consciousness, all the major concerns that you have with your current project.

This could include:

- Research issues.
- Plot holes.
- Problematic characters.
- Writerly concerns.
- Self-doubt.
- General inconsistencies.

Come back to this tomorrow. Taking each problem at a time, come up with practical solutions and start to make necessary changes or progress to rectify each one.

Day Fifteen

The Beyond Task

Free to Be

Find a magazine. Choose an image of a person. Free-write for ten minutes, in stream-of-consciousness style.

Try not to think about it too much. It doesn't matter if you fly from rich physical description into a poetic interior monologue. Just splurge. Enjoy exploring the character inside and out.

The Extra Task

Out of Control

List the events in your story that are out of the control of your protagonist but are affecting their actions throughout.

Set a timer for five minutes. For each event at a time, write your protagonist's state of mind. Vary form: for instance, one response could be in the form of a haiku, another could be in the form of an exam answer.

Continue for five minutes for each response. If time allows, try this with other characters.

Day Sixteen

The Beyond Task

Big Little Ideas

Quickly invent a character. Write one or two sentences about them.

Write a brief response to these questions:

- What motivates that character? (i.e. what is their goal?)
- What incident created this goal?
- What obstacles and events will they face in opposition to their ambitions?
- How will this be resolved?

For 15 minutes, write an opening page or so for this story.

The Extra Task

Mentors

Which characters in your novel serve as your protagonist's and antagonist's closest confidants? What would these characters tell the hero and villain about each other? Do they have a different perspective? How would they advise them to resolve their issues for the best possible outcome?

Write two flash fiction pieces, of no more than 1000 words, from the mentor's point of view regarding the conflict between the two major characters.

Day Seventeen

The Beyond Task

Choose Your Own Story

Read the opening paragraph from a novel. Write two paragraphs to follow on that take the story in a different direction. You could:

- Change the character's motivation.
- Add an element from a different genre.
- Add in details from a recent news story you have heard about.

The Extra Task

Unexpected Bonus

Choose a chapter that you have already written. What would happen if, in the middle of the action, one of the characters were to receive £10000?

Rewrite a plot outline for the chapter with the windfall included. If money was not a barrier to that character, how would it change the story? Would they be able to use the money to solve a problem? Would it change power and dynamics between characters? Would it make major changes to the character's personality? Does that reinforce any decisions you have already made about their actions and role?

Day Eighteen

The Beyond Task

Alternate Universe

Write a sonnet about a decision you have had to make but write it as if you made the other choice.

A sonnet is 14 lines long, written in iambic pentameter (10 syllables, alternating a rise and fall), and follows an ABAB CDCD EFEF GG rhyme scheme.

The Extra Task

Knowledge is Control

Choose at least three books from your bookshelf, fiction or non-fiction, (or visit the local library if you have more time) that you think would be good to read for research on your own novel. Read for as long as you can spare. Make notes along the way and include details of how and why that relates to your own work.

Day Nineteen

The Beyond Task

Tense

Choose one of these tenses:

PAST	PRESENT	FUTURE
Past Simple e.g. We watched a film.	Present simple e.g. I watch a film.	Future simple e.g. I will watch a film.
Past continuous e.g. I had watched a film	Present continuous e.g. I am watching a film.	Future continuous e.g. I will be watching a film.
Past perfect e.g. I had watched a film.	Present perfect e.g. I have watched a film.	Future perfect e.g. I will have watched a film.
Past perfect continuous e.g. I had been watching a film.	Present perfect continuous e.g. I have been watching a film.	Future perfect continuous e.g. I will have been watching a film.

Now choose your favourite fairy tale and rewrite it in the tense you have chosen.

The Extra Task

Questions and Answers

Many characters in your novel will have a raison d'être. For each character, write a question that pertains to this. For example, 'Will Beauty fall in love with the Beast?' and then write the answer, including as many details as you can to build a picture of how they will move, grow, and change throughout the novel. These are your round characters.

In contrast you may find that some of the characters stay the same throughout. They may help to move the narrative forward but ultimately do not undergo any major changes or revelations. These are your flat characters.

Day Twenty

The Beyond Task

Not All Quite as it Seems

Practice symbolism using your story from day five ('Knock, Knock'). For instance, an object, situation, name, or action can be used as a symbol to represent something else within the narrative that adds layers and texture to the meaning of a story.

What do you think could be a symbol in the story? Where could you add symbolism in what you've already written? What else could you write? For instance, you could add something to the door that alludes to the character. Or maybe the first thing that they see when it is opened represents something that has happened, or could happen to them in the future.

The Extra Task

Letters to You

Write yourself a letter from one of your minor characters. Let them tell you what they are thinking about what is happening in the novel, what they want to happen, how they think things could change, and what they are fearful of.

Day Twenty-One

The Beyond Task

Sniffing it Out

What was the last smell you noticed? Was it in your kitchen, a person you were sat next to on the bus, or maybe in an unfamiliar place?

List all the words that you can think of that describe the smell. Be evocative, be thoughtful, and be bold. Smell is a sense that human beings tend to take for granted.

Spend five minutes writing about the smell. Describe it, show a reader what the smell symbolises, and the journey that it takes you on.

The Extra Task

Turning

From memory, jot down the points in your work where a change occurs. This could be an action, a conversation, a conflict, a new character, or a choice made.

Write down a few thoughts about each turning point, whether you have already written the scene or not. Amongst your own reflections, ask yourself the following:

- Will/does the scene move the plot forward?
- Are there any issues with how A gets to B? What are they? Why do you think there is an issue?
- Does this change occur at the right point in the novel?
- Is this a minor, or major, climax within the novel?

Day Twenty-Two

The Beyond Task

Short and Sweet

Choose a word.

You have another 299 words. Allowing yourself only those 299 words, write a short story, using your chosen word as the springboard. Right now.

The Extra Task

Set the Scene

Plan out your next chapter with the following framework:

- Location: Where? Ten words/ideas to describe it.
- Characters: Who is there? List the following: Central character, round characters, flat characters.
- Sequence of events: Each scene within the chapter.
- Significant action/reaction/event: What needs to happen in this chapter, and why?

What next?

The Beyond Task

Three to Win

Choose three of these words:

Crusader	Flaunt	Masterpiece
Fleeting	Subsequent	Collapsed
Morsels	Arid	Laudable
Cove	Hostile	Among
Forcefully	Extravagant	Peach
Cog	Palettes	District
Chauffeur	Exodus	Deal
Sector	West	Jester
Confine	Decode	Bombshell

Use these three words to write a paragraph.

Pick three more. Write another paragraph.

Choose a final three. Write a closing paragraph.

The Extra Task

Back to the Beginning

Reread your work in progress from the very beginning. Highlight anything that suddenly seems like a bad idea.

Leave it to sit, but keep those highlighted missteps in mind as you move forward with your writing.

Day Twenty-Four

The Beyond Task

Looking In

Look up/out/around. Write one sentence to describes that image.

How are you feeling? Write one sentence that describes that emotion.

Now write a sentence where that emotion is part of that image.

Now write a sentence that displaces that emotion within the image.

The Extra Task

Out Loud

Read your most recent work out loud. Now go back and read aloud the dialogue only.

Is it obvious which character is speaking when? If yes, why? What have you given to each character's voice to add depth to their dialogue?

If no, what could you do to bring their spoken words to life? What could the way that they speak show a reader about who they are? Perhaps one of them has an accent or an unusual inflection. Or maybe the way they speak provides clues to who is talking and when. Do they ask lots of questions? Are they fond of long, unfathomably intricate words? Maybe they say, 'mate,' at the end of every sentence, or have a habit of stopping mid-sentence.

Note down some ideas of how your main players speak. Think about the tone and texture of voices in real life conversations. Rewrite the dialogue that you have just read using the qualities of those real-life chatterboxes to bring your dialogue – and characters – to life.

Day Twenty-Five

The Beyond Task

It's Your Story Now

Pick a random book from your bookshelf and open it on any page. Choose a paragraph. Rewrite that paragraph in as many ways as you can.

The Extra Task

Behind the Scenes

For as many characters as you wish, write a page that unfolds their back story.

Now create a table with two columns, titled 'Relevant' and 'Irrelevant' respectively. Dissect each point you have described in their back story and decide whether it serves a purpose within your narrative, assigning it to the applicable column.

Day Twenty-Six

The Beyond Task

A View of One's Own

Write no more than three paragraphs to describe the view from a window in your home from memory.

The Extra Task

What's Your Question?

We have already spent time looking at the motivation for your characters. But what about you? What question are you trying to answer with this story?

Use your writing journal to write a new diary entry, as freely-written as you like, to consider the major themes in your work.

The next time you reread your own work, bear this central idea in mind, and consider how successfully the events you have created seek to settle these ideas.

Day Twenty-Seven

The Beyond Task

Stranger Danger

Pick five of these attributes:

Clammy	Wheezing	Cropped	Sweaty	Formal
Beard	Athletic	Protruding	Jittery	Hopeful
Calm	Leathery	Jubilant	Hat	Beautiful
Eager	Confused	Rampant	Flaky	Glazed

A stranger knocks at your door and asks, 'Can I come in?' Before you answer, you look them up and down.

Using the five words that you have chosen, write a physical description of them. Think about what those details say about them and how that can build into their character.

Sleight of Hand

Choose three pages from your own work. Highlight every adjective and adverb that you have used in the section. Are they all necessary to the plot, or could some disappear without changing the meaning? Say, 'Goodbye' to them.

Next, go through and highlight again, this time with a focus on your -ing words. Get rid of the -ings. For example, 'He was kicking the football,' becomes, 'He kicked the football." Focus on creating the tightest prose possible.

Day Twenty-Eight

The Beyond Task

Blindfolded

Make a choice: rural or urban?

Now choose a location that represents your choice.

Make a choice: day or night?

Now imagine you are being walked through that situation blindfolded. Use your sense of smell and hearing to describe what you think is going on around you.

The Extra Task

Pick Your Own Battles

Create your own versions of the following table to detail the conflicts that will be faced in your novel. If you have two characters at war, consider the reasons and emotions for both sides.

Conflict: *(Include details of the conflict and what caused it)*			
Who does it affect?			
Why does it affect them?			
Emotional response			

Day Twenty-Nine

The Beyond Task

All the Words in the World

Write down the first five words that you think of. Now write down a new word next to each which you feel is associated with that word.

Now write down as many ways to say the words in your second list as you can think of. Spend around two minutes per word.

The Extra Task

Where is the Love?

Take your paired characters, from those already in a relationship to those that are denying their feelings for each other.

For each pair, write about their relationship. Go in to as much detail as you like. Write love poems from one to the other, think about the way they interact in the novel, why they love each other, and why they sometimes hate each other.

Now write down the reasons why these pairings are important to your work, and how the relationship plays into the plot. Is it a subplot? The ultimate goal? A convenient device? What would happen if you were to break a couple apart, or never get them together? Would it change the story?

The Beyond Task

Portals

Write down three films or television series that you know well. Take the hero from the first, the villain from the second, and the main setting/world from the last.

Write a plot outline for a story that would involve the hero and villain facing off in their new world.

The Extra Task

The In Between

Using either your novel plan, or the work you have already written, write down the things that would happen in the empty spaces between the events that end one chapter and begin another. Make notes about your characters' emotions, what could change from one moment to the next, and how they might behave immediately following those events or how they would decide to act as they do in the upcoming scene.

Day Thirty-One

The Beyond Task

Trailing Off Mid-Sentence

Turn the TV on. The first seven words you hear are your sentence starter. Now turn it back off and write for ten minutes.

The Extra Task

Happily Ever Afters

Wherever you are in the writing stage, write the closing paragraph for your story. Obviously, this doesn't have to be the ending at all, but sometimes knowing exactly where you're going to can help you to stay focussed on getting there.

6

FOUNDATIONS

You've made it. How do you feel? Ready to do it all over again?

In all of life it is important to appreciate and work hard for the now. Make your goal to make a success of your current situation. It's not a case of, 'where can I go next?' or 'I want...' - if you want to move forward, embrace what you can achieve right now. That's how we reach the whens and ifs that we daydream about. They may not always be quite what we hoped for – or expected – but they are our progression through life all the same.

What you do today will bring moments of mistakes and times of accomplishment. *Beyond Habit* is here to be part of your writing process now, whenever that now is. We all have our writing dreams, I know that better than anyone, but I truly believe that the most success I can ever ask for in one given moment is to put one miraculous word in front of another to write the best damn tale that I can. And hopefully practice will help to make that a reality for all of us.